ADVANCE PRAISE FOR
Self-Motivated Kids

"A smart, practical book for moms and dads who care about their kids' intrinsic motivation!"

—Daniel H. Pink, Bestselling author of DRIVE and A WHOLE NEW MIND

"Every parent struggles to help their children become more self-motivated. Simmons shares some crucial concepts and great implementation tips to help parents do just that. Wish I had this with my kids but glad I have it for my grandkids! This is very clear, do-able, and inspiring! The 3 Cs are life changing!"

—Merilee Boyack, author of THE PARENTING BREAKTHROUGH

"A practical and quick read, perfect for busy parents. The 3-C's are a must! Simmons covers connection, competence, choice, communication, transitions, and routines all in a way that is practical and easy to implement. She presents motivation theory in a way that will not only help children develop internal motivation, but that will also build a positive relationship between parents and children. If you have a toddler or a teen, this is a great read for all parents!"

—Ashley Soderlund Ph.D., creator of NurtureandThriveBlog.com

"Self-Motivated Kids is a practical resource for parents who are looking for positive alternatives to threats, bribes and yelling."

—Nicole Schwarz, LMFT, creator of ImperfectFamilies.com

"Self-Motivated Kids offers a powerful and mercifully succinct guide to us parents in the thick of raising littles. Even those of us aware of and committed to peaceful parenting need to continuously course correct, establish and re-establish mindful parenting practices. With a focus on feeding children's intrinsic motivation, Simmons unearths key practices that are both realistic and actionable to activate our children's innate desire to collaborate with us."

—Avital, creator of TheParentingJunkie.com

"This book is a MUST READ! As an educator, I cannot count the number of times I have heard parents say, "If only my son/daughter came with a handbook!" Simmons uses her experience as a family life educator and mom to create 'the handbook.'"

—Stacey Sly, author of TRAUMA IN THE CLASSROOM

"This is the perfect book for a reflective parent. If you are looking for the tools and insight to help you achieve a positive, deep, and lasting relationship with your children, while teaching them to be self-sufficient in a positive manner, this book will help you."

—Jessaca Olsen, mother of two

"When I returned from my last deployment, I realized I needed to figure out how to be a parent. The principles in this book rang true to me. They are similar ideas to how we lead and develop Marines, but the book put it in a way that I could use the concepts as a parent."

—Capt Kevin Stephensen (USMC)

"I love, love, LOVED this book! I will be trying out lots of things and will keep you posted on how they work!"

—Jessica Meek, **mother of five**

"I have been using the three Cs with my kids and have noticed a night-and-day difference in their behavior. I find myself enjoying parenting more because I am able to connect with my kids and see how happy they are when they get to choose something or…accomplish something new."

—Shianne Healey, **mother of two**

"Many parenting books are overwhelming, but not this one! I really like the "Take Action" section and questions at the end of each chapter, as they help me reflect and make immediate changes to better my parenting. This book actually makes me excited to be a mom and use these tools to help my children become self-motivated as they grow!"

—Stephanie Davis, **mother of five**

This book is perfect for the parent who feels like they need a little extra help and motivation to make it through their day. As a mother of two, I have read this book and put Simmons' ideas and parenting concepts into practice. I have seen a difference in our day-to-day living. Our home is happier because we have implemented these ideas.

—Nicole Burnham, **mother of two**

Self-Motivated
KIDS

CREATING AN ENVIRONMENT WHERE CHILDREN

LISTEN AND COOPERATE

Damara Simmons

Self-Motivated KIDS

CREATING AN ENVIRONMENT WHERE CHILDREN LISTEN AND COOPERATE

Damara Simmons

Creator of ParentingBrilliantly.com

**COPYRIGHT © 2016 – Step By Step, LLC.
ALL RIGHTS RESERVED.**

No part of this publication may be reproduced, distributed, or transmitted in any form or by any means, including, but not limited to, photocopying, recording, or other electronic or mechanical methods, without prior written permission of the publisher, except in the case of brief quotations embodied in critical reviews and certain other noncommercial uses permitted by copyright law.

For permission request, write to the publisher at "Attention Permissions Coordinator" at the address below.

**216 Misty Valley Lane, Bonaire GA 31005
Damara@ParentingBrilliantly.com**

Important Disclaimer

This publication contains materials designed to assist parents with their children's motivation and is for education purposes only. While the publisher and author have made every attempt to verify that the information provided in this is book is correct, the publisher and author assume no responsibility for any error, inaccuracy, or omission. The advice, examples, and strategies contained herein are not suitable for every situation. The materials contained herein are not intended to represent or guarantee you will achieve your desired results, and the publisher and author make no such guarantee. Neither the publisher nor author shall be liable for damages arising therefrom. Success is determined by a number of factors beyond the control of the publisher and author, including, but not limited to, child's developmental level, temperament, effort level, and time. You understand every parent and child is unique.

Ordering Information

Quantity sales. Special discounts are available on quantity purchases by corporations, associations, and others. For details, contact the publisher at the address below.

216 Misty Valley Lane, Bonaire GA 31005
Damara@ParentingBrilliantly.com

ISBN-13: 978-1539917823

ISBN-10: 1539917827

Self-Motivated KIDS: CREATING AN ENVIRONMENT WHERE CHILDREN LISTEN AND COOPERATE

Damara Simmons

1. Parenting. 2. Parent and child. 3. Child rearing. 4. Motivation

Editing by Sarah Monson
Book Cover Design by Julie Brew Finlayson
Illustrations by Rudie Strummer

7 Days to Self-Motivated Kids

THE SECRET IS OUT....

You can create a home environment where your children listen and cooperate. How is this done? It is surprisingly simple:

Meet your child's 3 basic psychological needs.

Self-Motivated Kids has a free companion e-course that outlines these needs in a three-step approach. The magic occurs when you stop trying to control your children and start adjusting the environment in your home.

This step-by-step course teaches: 1) How to avoid unhealthy parenting practices that manipulate children and cause the negative behaviors that drive you crazy. 2) How to meet your children's three psychological needs so they listen and respond. 3) How to communicate with children so they are motivated from within—all on their own.

To stop feeling overwhelmed and get the parenting support you need, use the following link to reserve your spot:

SelfMotivatedKids.com/step1

Dedicated to

My **PARENTS**, *for* giving me a start in life…

My **HUSBAND**, *for* believing in me…

My **SONS**, *for* being my inspiration…

And to **YOU**, *for* giving it a try.

Contents

7 Days to Self-Motivated Kids 8
Dedicated to 9
Introduction: My Story 11

Part One: Motivation

Carrots and Sticks 16
Fueling Self-Motivation 24
The Environment 30

Part Two: Creating the Environment

Connection is No. 1 40
The Power of Choice 50
Competence 62

Part Three: The Magic Formula

The Power of Three 74
Close, Quiet, Connect 80
What You *Can* Do 90

"The Why" Matters 98
Routines Reduce Friction 106
Transitions Allow Space 118
Engaging Questions 126

Part Four: Where to Start

The Gift of Today 136
Don't Take My Word for It 140

Where Do You Go From Here? 143
Self-Motivated Kids Companion Course ... 145
Additional Parenting Resources 146
Acknowledgements 150
About the Author 153
Notes 154

Introduction: My Story

In 1999 I gave birth to my first child. (Whew! What an experience!) As I cradled my wee babe in my arms, a wildfire of emotions rushed through me. Love, panic, excitement, nervousness, exhaustion and joy consumed my heart and mind.

After a few days of hospital food (yuck) and air-conditioned gowns (double yuck), I was ecstatic when my doctor signed our release. My husband and I were thrilled as we drove home. Once we were situated, my husband looked at me with a blank expression. "Now what?" he asked.

I looked at him, and down at our swaddled son and then back at my husband. *Oh, no! Oh, no!* My brain screamed, *how can we do this? Why did we ever think we could be parents?*

Seventeen years have passed since we stepped into the unknown. Throughout those years, I have searched for light to illuminate the darkness of inexperience.

One of my biggest challenges was how to communicate so my children would listen and cooperate. I talked to many parents, read dozens of books, dug into the latest research, conducted my own informal interviews, and prayed often, trying to find the answers.

My search led me to the idea of motivation, and more specifically, self-motivation. I was curious: where did self-motivation come from? How could I instill it in my children? Were there ways to motivate without manipulation? And how do I create a home environment where my children could be self-motivated?

As I continued to study parenting strategies and ways to communicate, I made adjustments in my own parenting and saw dramatic results. I knew I had discovered something important—extremely important.

In this book, I lovingly share my insights and discoveries with you, a parent who knows there must be a better way.

Part One:
Motivation

01

Carrots and Sticks

There are only two ways to influence human behavior; you can manipulate it or you can inspire it.

— *Simon Sinek*

"Stop it or else!"

"If I have to tell you again, you're in timeout!"

"You can have a cookie if you eat your veggies."

"Because I said so!"

"If you clean your room, I'll pay you a dollar."

"You're going to be in so much trouble with your dad!"

"Hurry up! You're making us late!"

"If you don't get your homework done, I'm taking your phone!"

Have you ever caught yourself saying some of these phrases? I know I have. What about parenting methods like glaring, pinching, spanking, pushing, slapping, and grabbing? So what exactly is the purpose behind these actions and comments?

Simply said, they are attempts to *motivate* your children.

However, most parents don't realize these threats, bribes, punishments, and physical harm actually create more problems than they solve.

Why is that?

These parenting methods cause children to be fearful, anxious, less capable, filled with shame, and more resistant. When children experience these difficult emotions, they will often behave *worse*!

Here is a personal example. When my son Stephen was five years old, I signed up to be his soccer coach. During one of the games, he asked to come out for a break. I motioned him over and sent in our only sub, informing Stephen to rest until someone else needed a break. A few minutes later, another exhausted player asked to come out—but Stephen refused to go in. The angrier I got, the more resistant he became. After threatening all sorts of punishments, I realized I was making the situation worse! But here's the kicker...I didn't know what else to do.

As a mother and certified family life educator, I felt compelled to dig deeper into this motivation problem. I searched through the latest research and interviewed parents and children. And I was amazed by what I discovered.

But first, we need to know where the motivation methods like punishments, bribes, and threats originated. And how did these methods seep into our parenting?

History of Motivation

Centuries ago, when food and safety were less certain, our ancestors' primary motivation was survival. In his insightful book *Drive,* author Daniel Pink refers to this basic motivation to survive as Motivation 1.0.[1]

Then around the time of the Industrial Revolution, as communities developed and the quality of life improved, humans were no longer forced to focus on mere survival. They didn't toil day after day in the blazing sun or the freezing snow to hunt, gather or farm; they began to take specialized jobs in factories and office buildings. In these settings, the following assumption developed among bosses and supervisors: *In order to motivate humans, they either need external rewards or punishments.*

And so the classic "carrot and stick" system was born. This system is based on extrinsic (external) motivation and employs bribes and incentives (carrots) or the threat of punishment (stick). When a worker did something right, he earned a reward. If he failed, he was punished. Pink refers to this system as Motivation 2.0:

The Motivation 2.0 operating system has endured for a very long time. Indeed, it is so deeply embedded in our lives that most of us scarcely recognize that it exists. For as long as any of us can remember, we've configured our organizations and constructed our lives around its bedrock assumption: The way to improve performance, increase productivity, and encourage excellence is to reward the good and punish the bad.[2]

Society has functioned under this assumption for hundreds of years, maybe longer. It influences the way businesses run, how schools function, and it *permeates the daily interaction of families.*

Although the carrot and stick method have been used for generations, it causes negative effects on children (both in the short term and long term).

Negative Effects

1. The more we use carrots and sticks, the *bigger* they need to become.

2. Carrots, and especially sticks, cause physical, emotional, and/or psychological harm.

3. Self-motivation shuts down when we use extrinsic carrots and sticks.

4. This method *increases* undesirable behaviors in our children.

5. Carrots and sticks trigger the reactive brain and block higher-level thinking.

Bigger and Bigger

The more parents use external motivation, the bigger the carrot and stick have to grow to remain effective. Imagine a four-year-old who is offered a quarter to take out the trash. How much will he want to be paid when he is eight? What will he expect when he turns twelve? The amount tends to continually grow bigger and bigger.

When parents use the carrot and stick approach, they have to keep *upping the ante* to motivate their kids.

Harmful

Using carrots and sticks harm children and inflict fear. This is especially true with physical and verbal punishments. Simon Sinek, author of *Start with Why* reports this insight, "Fear, real or perceived, is arguably the most powerful manipulation of the lot."[3]

Punishments sever relationships, diminish trust, and cause children harmful physical, psychological, and emotional pain that can last their entire lives.

This pain in children is *expressed through their undesirable behaviors* (aka whining, tantrums, back-talk, and noncooperation); which parents might counter with more physical, psychological, or emotional punishment. And so this sad, harmful spiral continues, around and around.

Shuts Down Self-Motivation

The definition of self-motivation is "the ability to independently complete what needs to be done." An example of this is a young child getting himself dressed or a teenager completing her homework without reminders.

However, the carrot and stick method *actually diminishes self-motivation* because children rely on the external motivation of the carrot and stick to complete tasks instead of autonomously finishing what needs to be done. Their focus is on the bribe or punishment instead of the internal ability or value of completing the task.

Again, think of the child who is paid to take out the trash. Is he self-motivated to help and be a contributing member of his family, or is he externally motivated by the money?

Fuels Bad Behavior

Children have a basic psychological need to feel *competent, connected, and autonomous*.[4] Unfortunately, when the carrot and stick method is used, children feel manipulated, coerced, pressured, and controlled. This in turn causes them to experience feelings of sadness, annoyance, hopelessness, and anger.

As a result, children express these feelings through negative behaviors which may include hitting, yelling, throwing fits, ignoring, and noncooperation—the exact behaviors loving parents are *trying to teach their children to avoid!*

Blocks Higher Thinking

When sticks are used on children, their reactive brain is triggered, sending them into fight, flight, or freeze mode. When children are experiencing any of these emotions, they cannot access their higher-level thinking brain where they are able to problem solve, creatively explore solutions or self-regulate their emotions.

Simply said, they are experiencing a state of stress which they communicate through tantrums or rebellion—the exact behaviors parents want stopped, but unknowingly cause. And so this vicious cycle continues.

The Cost

Unfortunately, the carrot and stick method *does* get results; but at what cost? Shutting down your children's self-motivation? Requiring a bigger and bigger carrot or stick? Causing physical or emotional harm to your children? Triggering more undesirable behaviors for you to continue battling?

Because the carrot and stick motivational method has been around for centuries, most parents have no idea what alternatives exist. Often, less-effective parenting methods are passed from one generation to the next.

Stacey Sly, a behavior interventionist and author of *Trauma in the Classroom,* explains that every parent wants what is best for their child but, "Wanting what is best for

[your] child does not mean [you] have the tools to provide it."[5]

Think of the interactions you have had with your children over the past 24 hours. Did you need to remind them dozens of times to complete homework or chores? Did you resort to yelling? Did you bribe them to get something done? Did you threaten them to finish? Did you lecture your teenager? Did you shake your fist and ask, "Why is this so hard?"

If you answered yes to any of these questions, *the way out is to stop using the carrot and stick method,* and, instead, start employing effective techniques that fuel self-motivation.

02

Fueling Self-Motivation

Motivation is the energy for action.

Motivation gets us up in the morning,

puts us to bed at night,

and does everything in between.

—**Dr. Edward Deci**

A mother of three was stretched beyond her limits. Her children seemed to regularly act out and throw fits at every corner. She constantly told them to "stop being naughty" and "behave." They rarely listened, so she resorted to yelling. This only left her feeling guilty and hopeless.

When they yelled and fought with each other, she threatened them with timeouts. Her two-year-old son seemed to be in timeout constantly, but his behavior didn't improve (in fact it seemed to make it worse).

She enrolled her kids in multiple activities to keep them busy and "out of trouble." Then one night, out of anger, she spanked her four-year-old because he kept getting out of bed. Later she collapsed, sobbing. Her heart ached, her head pounded; she was exhausted and out of ideas. If only they would listen and behave! "What on earth is wrong with them?" she called out heavenward.

Through the years, she talked to other parents, took classes, and read many books. She knew she needed a better way. First, she eliminated a few of the extra-curricular activities to *reduce her stress* and impatience. Then she began spending *quality connection time* with her children. Next she created a *dependable routine* that made their lives more predictable. Instead of raising her voice or yelling, she chose to *get close* to her children and *calmly explain* what they needed to do.

Slowly she made adjustments to the way she communicated and interacted with her children. And the results were magical! Her children actually listened (most of the time). They were happier and cooperated more often. Their motivation skyrocketed and their behavior improved dramatically. She finally felt like she was being the mother she wanted to be.

This is a true story—it is *my* story. I was a mess. I was constantly reacting to all of my kids' negative behaviors: whining, fighting, complaining, or back-biting. I felt guilty whenever I lost my cool. And I sensed the problem was me, but I didn't know what else to do.

What I discovered through my research is that human behavior stems from our *met or unmet needs*. These needs are buried deep within each of us and move us to action. This is the foundation for motivation—or the lack of it.

I also discovered that children want to cooperate! They want to listen! (Yes, you read that right; it is not a typo). So what gets in the way? *Their unmet needs*.

Human Needs

The most basic human needs are the physical ones that our bodies require in order to survive. These include food, safety (shelter and warmth), and rest. Parents are generally aware of their children's physical needs and regularly meet them.

However, few of us fully understand our basic human emotional and psychological needs. And even fewer know how to effectively communicate them to others. Doctors Edward L. Deci and Richard M. Ryan, who have researched motivation for more than 30 years, explain these needs in their Self-Determination Theory (SDT), which teaches that all humans have the psychological need to feel *competence, autonomy,* and *relatedness*[6].

This means your children must experience *feelings of accomplishment.* They need to be self-governing, empowered with the ability to *make personal life choices.* And they need to be *connected* to others so they feel love and belonging. These needs reside at the deepest core of their beings.

Researchers have proven that motivation (the ability to do what needs to be done) flourishes when these needs are met and respected. Having these needs met *fuels self-motivation* or, as Pink dubbed it, "Motivation 3.0."[7]

What does this mean?

When you meet your children's basic needs of competency, autonomy, and relatedness, *positive emotions* are triggered. These include feelings of happiness, contentment, inspiration, comfort, and love. When children experience these positive emotions, their higher-level thinking is activated. They solve problems more easily, experience increased creativity, make positive contributions, enjoy learning, willingly cooperate and listen. In summary, *they become self-motivated*!

Look at it this way: when a plant is watered, has enough nutrients, and receives ample sunlight, it grows. We don't have to poke, prod, or hurt it. When its needs are being met it grows—all on its own.

Self-motivated children don't have to be bribed or threatened to cooperate; they choose it on their own! *For themselves!*

What about you? Do you want children who listen and cooperate? Who enjoy learning, proactively finish tasks on their own, work through problems, and make positive contributions to your family? If your answer is a resounding yes, then the key is creating an *environment* where self-motivated kids can grow.

Damara Simmons

03

The Environment

I've learned how one tweak in the environment changes everything.
—**Marshall Goldsmith**

"When you plant lettuce, if it does not grow well, you don't blame the lettuce. You look into reasons it is not doing well."[8] *That's interesting,* I muse. *This lettuce analogy sounds like a parallel to parenting.*

I glance back at my book, *Peace Is Every Step* by Thich Nhat Hanh, "It may need fertilizer, or more water, or less sun. You never blame the lettuce. Yet if we have problems with our friends or our family, we blame the other person." Again I pause. *This really does relate to parenting. <u>Instead of blaming our children for problems, we need to make adjustments in the way we treat them and talk to them.</u> This is like adjusting the amounts of fertilizer, water, and sun for the lettuce.*

"But if we know how to take care of them," the book continues, "they will grow well, like lettuce." *Yes,* I muse, *if we know how to take care of our children, they too, will grow well.*

Thich Nhat Hanh's lettuce analogy shed light on a truth I had already discovered. Similar to his garden environment, parents can create a *home environment* where children thrive and where they are motivated to listen and cooperate—all on their own.

Dr. Edward Deci shares in his TEDx talk that motivation exists in everyone. However, he points out the *conditions* around us influence whether we are self-motivated.[9] This means when parents create the correct conditions that foster an environment of self-motivation, children can't help but be motivated.

The Three Cs

What can you do to create this environment of self-motivation? Meet your children's three core psychological needs of connection, choice, and competence. It's that simple. When all three of these needs are met, children *automatically* become more self-motivated.

To help you remember these three core needs of connection, choice, and competence, we will simply call them the three Cs. Throughout this book, you will see them listed inside a diagram of a house. This symbolizes the home environment you are creating.

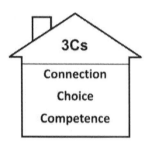

So what exactly do connection, choice and competence mean? Here is a brief overview of each one:

Connection

Children need to feel acceptance, belonging, and love. They need a safe place where they can seek refuge from the storms of life; a place where they are wrapped in arms of protection and security. They need to feel connected to other human beings. While they are young, they especially *need to feel connected to you.*

In his book *Social*, Matthew D. Lieberman, a professor at UCLA, shares this insight about the importance of social connection:

It shouldn't be surprising to us that being social is essential to our well-being. Everything we have learned about the social brain tells us that we are wired to make and keep social connections, that we feel pain when these connections are threatened, and that our identity, our sense of self, is intimately tied up with the groups we are a part of.[10]

Children feel this need for connection, they too are wired for it. Their individual identities and sense of self are closely tied to their parents. They feel immense pain when this connection is threatened.

A child's need for connection is similar to Thich Nhat Hanh's lettuce needing water to survive. When you create a home environment where children feel they *belong and matter,* they will more than survive, they will grow and thrive.

Choice

Choice gives children the personal feelings of control and power. Dr. Deci and Dr. Ryan refer to this as autonomy[11], or self-governing, which is the ability to make life choices.

Dr. Sue Grossman, a professor of early childhood education at Eastern Michigan University, neatly sums it up this way: "Our task is to provide children with appropriate, healthful options…In this way, we are developing confident, independent children who feel in control of themselves."[12]

Choices are similar to the various types of fertilizers (natural or manmade) Thich Nhat Hanh's lettuce needs to receive essential nutrients. Likewise, children need to make age-appropriate choices and be involved in decision making so they can grow into self-governing, responsible adults. Only through making choices can children feel personal power in their lives.

Competence

Children also need to feel (and be) proficient in developmentally-appropriate skills. They long to know they are capable and can master more challenging tasks.

Dr. Jim Taylor, a University of San Francisco professor who specializes is the psychology of parenting shares,

Children crave opportunities to demonstrate their competence. They love to contribute and they love to do adult things. Why? Perhaps they are hard-wired to want to do what adults do [which] ensures that they learn what they need to survive as adults.[13]

At a young age, children want to be competent. If you watch a two-year-old who is determined to get dressed by himself, you see a child who longs for that feeling.

Competence is like the sunlight Thich Nhat Hanh's lettuce needs to make food for itself. Similarly, children need to experience feelings of competence as they accomplish new tasks, learn from mistakes, and develop personal independence.

The Environment

Just like Thich Nhat Hanh, we don't blame the lettuce—or the children—if things aren't working. Instead, we make adjustments to the environment (water, fertilizer, and sunlight).

Likewise, instead of blaming our children for problems, we need to make adjustments to our home environments. We do this by meeting our children's need for connection, choice, and competence on a *daily basis*. This means adjusting the way we treat our children and communicate with them.

When their needs are met, children feel cared for, nurtured, capable, and confident. These positive emotions activate their higher-level thinking, which means they solve problems more easily, experience increased creativity, make positive contributions, enjoy learning, and more willingly listen and cooperate.

In summary, when children have their three basic psychological needs met, they *can't help* but be self-motivated. They listen and cooperate because they *want to,* not because they are nagged, threaten, bribed, or punished.

This diagram summarizes how an environment of self-motivation can be created in your home.

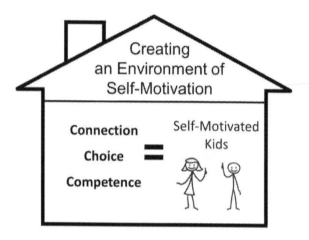

So how do you specifically meet your child's need for connection, choice, and competence? How do you raise children who have the energy for action? How do you create this environment of self-motivation?

Let's head over to Part II: Creating the Environment, where you will discover parenting behaviors that *impede* an environment of self-motivation, what kids have to say, and a summary of strategies you can immediately start using to *create* an environment of self-motivation.

Damara Simmons

Self-Motivated Kids

Part Two:
Creating the Environment

04

Connection is No. 1

Beautiful, priceless moments of connection do not happen if we are constantly on the go.

—**Rachel Macy Stafford**

"Come on, boys, we need to go! You're going to be late to swim practice!" I yell.

My youngest walks towards me. His feet are bare.

"Where are your shoes? You need your shoes! Seriously, you know what to do! Go get your shoes!"

I glance at tomorrow's schedule: Cub Scouts and piano lessons. The next day shows swim lessons and a church meeting. The following day there are two soccer practices and Boy Scouts. My head starts spinning.

Another month passes, and I grow more impatient, frustrated, and sometimes flat-out mean. My children listen less and bicker more.

Why are they behaving this way? Why are they not listening and cooperating? Don't they know I am doing all this for them?

During this time in our lives, as we rushed from one activity to another and my stress level rose, my children's motivation seemed to spiral downward.

I did not realize by over-scheduling our activities and under-scheduling needed connection time, their behavior was growing more resistant, causing me to feel more frustrated. This negative cycle was slowly whittling away at our relationship and their motivation.

Here are a few thoughts from children when they experience disconnect from their parent(s).

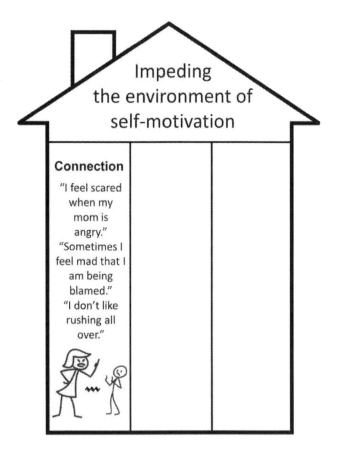

Children feel scared, overwhelmed, mad, frustrated, and resistant when they no longer think they matter. All of these feelings impede an environment of self-motivation. So what can we do instead?

Greg McKeown, bestselling author of *Essentialism,* explains:

There are far more activities and opportunities in the world than we have time and resources to invest in. And although many of them may be good, or even very good, the fact is that most are trivial and few are vital.[14]

My life was out of control. It was time to ask, "Are all these activities vital? And if they are not vital, what is?" As I thought about these questions, reflected on my behavior, and looked at my young children, I realized they did not need numerous extra activities—*they needed connection time with me.*

Connection is Spelled T-I-M-E

Before the 1900s, children often worked alongside their parents in fields, gardens, and homes. In this setting they had time to talk and share stories while parents taught life skills. Everything revolved around the family.

Today with the many obligations, extra-curricular activities, distractions, and constant pulls for our time, it is most important to prioritize time with our children. Dr. Shefali, a clinical psychologist and author of *Out of Control,* sums it up beautifully: "The first task of any parent is to establish connection."[15]

Scheduling time to spend together builds family connection and helps children experience feelings of love and belonging. Like Dr. Shefali explains, this is a parent's first task.

However, in our fast-paced, busy lives, it is challenging to make time to connect with our children. But it can be done.

In Travis Stephensen's inspiring book *Exploring Edges;* he shares his Ironman training experiences. One of his biggest concerns in undertaking such intensive training was the amount of time he would be away from his treasured family. Instead of giving up his goal, he bought a stationary bike and played video games or watched movies with his children as he pedaled away for hours.[16]

Like Stephensen, with a little creativity and brainstorming we can discover solutions to this T-I-M-E issue. We can carve out white space in our busy schedules to spend quality connection time with our children.

Where to Start

Review your weekly schedule together as a family. If you see there are multiple activities per child, per week, discuss where you can scale back a little to increase the opportunity for family connection. The activities you eliminate can free up time for conversations and activities together.

Ask your children what they would like to do. Brainstorm ideas and make a list. Here are a few suggestions to get you started:

Cook a meal.
Make a dessert.
Be silly together.
Play a game.
Talk about your day.
Hug each other.
Play sports.
Read books.
Build a project.
Tuck each child in at night.

Quality connection time can be scheduled or spontaneous. If you cannot free up time, make the most of the moments you have together. It is not important how it happens; only that it *does* happen. Two of the quickest, purest forms of connection is through a smile and hug.

Through my years of parenting and testing, I have also discovered that quality connection time can fall under one or all three of these categories: *laugh, listen, and learn.*

1. Children of all ages love to *laugh* and play. As a parent, don't take yourself too seriously. Be silly. Play and laugh often with your children, they will love you for it.
2. Children appreciate parents who don't just talk but truly *listen*. Take a few minutes to look your children in the eyes and really hear what they have to say.

3. Children are naturally curious so they enjoy *learning* new skills and ideas alongside you. Invite your children to work next to you as you complete chores and tasks around your home.

I interviewed children and asked if they enjoyed spending time with their families and, specifically, their parents. Here are a few of their comments:

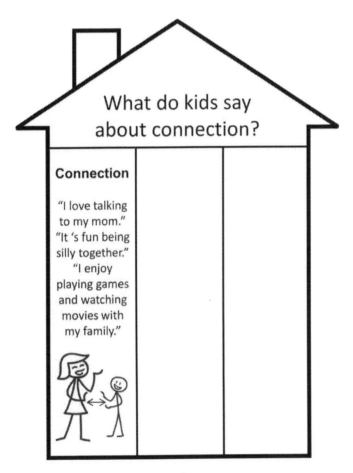

⌂ Creating the Environment

As I scaled back on our extra activities—and consciously increased our connection time—a shift happened in our home environment. I was less stressed and became more patient. My children's self-motivation increased when we no longer rushed around at a frantic pace. They became more attentive to what I said and willingly helped (most of the time) when asked. This shift towards connection changed our entire home for the better.

Connecting with your children is the first step in creating an environment of self-motivation. If you struggle with your children not listening and being non-cooperative, they are often craving connection. Meet this need by making time for them and connecting individually with each of your children on a daily basis.

When your children cooperate, are helpful, and listen, take a second to thank them. Let them know they make a difference and you appreciate their contribution. This increases connection.

As you hug, laugh, and spend quality time together, you are meeting your child's need for connection and are starting to *create an environment* of self-motivation. These times of togetherness will become treasured moments of love and joy.

> **TAKE ACTION:** If you have too many activities, decide which ones you can eliminate to enjoy quality connection time with your children.

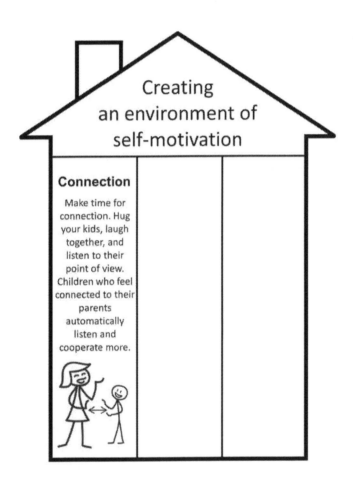

SELF-REFLECTION QUESTIONS:

1. *Do I live life at a frantic, crazy pace?*

2. *What side effects have resulted from this fast-paced living?*

3. *What can I eliminate from my schedule?*

4. *When can I spend a few minutes of connection time with my children each day?*

05

The Power of Choice

When we forget our ability to choose,

we learn to be helpless.

—**Greg McKeown**

"Here's a drink of milk," I say while handing my two-year-old son his cup.

"I want the blue cup! I want the blue cup!" he cries out.

"I already poured it in the red cup," I explain.

"I want the bluuuuue cup!" he whines.

Fireworks explode inside my head. "You have to use this cup. I already poured it," I blurt.

Defiantly, he looks up and throws it on the ground.

Battling moments like these can trigger thoughts such as, "It's my way or the highway!" Or, "I'm the parent. I'm in control, so you listen to me!" Of course, children perceive our feelings and choose to resist.

But taking on this defiant behavior can ignite big, red anger in us. And out of that anger, we might make hurtful comments or even cause harm. Our child, now put in place, is sad and upset—no longer willing (or able) to listen.

When did the problem in my scenario start? When I resisted my son's need to choose his cup. While this might seem silly to an adult, it is a big deal to a young child. They need to make life choices too—even small, seemingly insignificant ones.

When children are told all day long what to do, their need for autonomy screams out, "I want a choice in my life! I need to choose."

Imagine a day from your child's point of view and what they might hear:

"Get up–get dressed."

"Put these clothes on."

"You have to wear your coat."

"Eat your breakfast."

"Go to school"

"Do what your teacher says, or you'll get in trouble"

"Finish your homework."

"Clean your room."

"Take a bath."

"Read your book."

"Help your brother."

"Brush your teeth."

"Go to bed."

After being told what to do all day, a child's freewill bursts at the seams. He wants a say in his life. *He wants a choice.*

Here is what children say about feeling powerless:

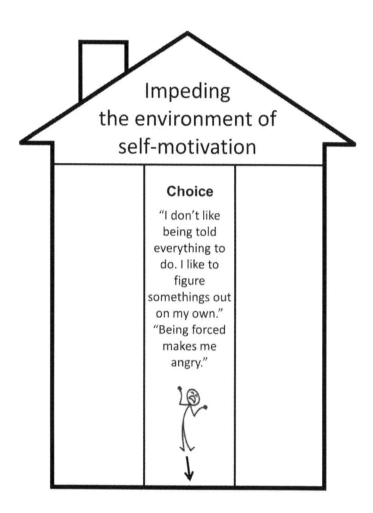

As you can see, children like to have some control in their lives. Yes, we are the parents and adults in the relationship, but as children grow we need to *slowly* shift decision-making responsibilities over to them. This allows them a chance to think on their own instead of constantly being told what to do. The key is giving age-appropriate choices and sharing control so children feel personal power in their lives. Let's take a look at how this is done.

Examples of Choices

You can give **young children** more autonomy by sharing your expectation and then offering two acceptable choices. Choices are most effective when children are calm (not tired or hungry) so they can think. Here are some examples.

Instead of:	*Say This:*
Time for a drink; here is your cup.	Time for a drink. Do you want the blue cup or green cup?
Hold my hand.	I need you to be safe. Do you want to hold my left hand or right hand?
We will read a book.	Time to read. Do you want to read one or two books?
Get dressed. Put on this shirt.	Time to get dressed. Do you want to wear the red shirt or the blue one?

Young children might struggle to make a choice. In these cases, remind them they can choose the other option another time. This reassures children they will have another chance. Now they can move forward with one option.

Elementary-aged children can handle more advanced choices that involve time. Again, explain what is expected and offer two acceptable choices.

Instead of:	*Say This:*
Turn off the game.	You need to finish your game. Would you like three minutes to wrap things up, or five?
Time to do your homework.	Homework needs to be finished before dinner. Do you want to do it now and then play; or play for 20 minutes and then finish your homework?
Clean your room and vacuum the living room.	Time to clean. Do you want to clean your room or vacuum first?

Many **teenagers** like to think of their own options. It is an important life skill to practice before they become adults.

Instead of offering choices, you can explain what is expected and then discuss what alternatives they have.

Instead of:	*Say This:*
Turn off your phone.	Where would you like to put your phone so you can focus?
Time to do your homework.	What is your plan for homework tonight?
Be home at 10:00	I need you home by 10:00. What are your plans?

Allowing teenagers to think through their different options and choose when to start or what they *can* do fulfills the need for choice.

Children of all ages like to make choices each day. Choices empower children to take action. McKeown explains, "We often think of choice as a thing. But a choice is not a thing. Our options may be things, but a choice—a choice is an *action*."[17]

When we give children choices, we are showing them the options they have and are inviting them to *take action* on one of them.

Giving Control

Children love choices. In my interviews, I asked children if they liked having choices. Most replied with a resounding yes! Here are a few of their comments:

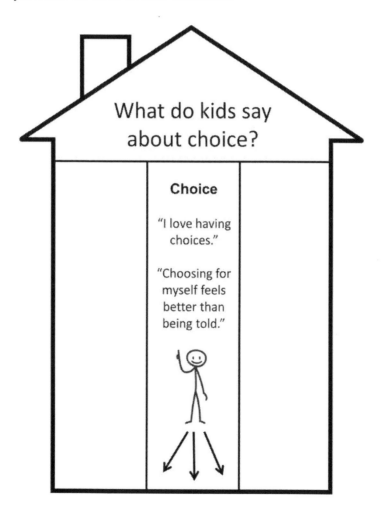

Recently, my son, who is in high school, explained that he is enjoying language arts for the first time. When I asked why he felt differently about it, he explained that his teacher gives the class choices about the projects they complete. Because the choices give him control over his own learning, he enjoys language arts and feels more motivated.

I asked a number of parents their thoughts about giving their children choices. Jessaca, a mother of a nineteen-year-old daughter and twenty-year-old son, shared these thoughts:

When my daughter was small, she was overwhelmed by choices, so I had to narrow it down for her. When kids choose, they feel better and have a buy-in in their lives.

Stephanie, a busy mother of five with children ranging from three to seventeen said:

I use choices as much as possible. I just used this one today: "You can clean your room quickly and have more time to play or take a long time and have less time to play. You choose." My kids love making decisions.

Explaining what needs to be done and then giving children two, age-appropriate choices offers them a "buy-in" and control in their lives. And, as Stephanie suggested, you can use choices to show children the natural outcomes of each choice.

⌂ Creating the Environment

When my son was young, it was important for him to pick the color of his cup, and I gave him the choice of two colors. As he grew older, I asked, "What cup do you want?" Now he can reach the cups and chooses on his own.

Giving my son the personal power of choice honors his need to be self-governing and encourages him to be self-motivated.

When your children seem resistant or battle against you, they need choices. Meet this need by telling them what needs to be done and give two acceptable choices or have a discussion with older children about their various options. And once your children make a choice, encourage them to move forward with their decision.

As you give your children a few choices each day, they will feel more autonomous. And their feelings of happiness will increase, resulting in more confident kids who have the energy for action. Giving choices and involving children in discussions is the second step in *creating an environment* of self-motivation.

TAKE ACTION: If you find yourself battling your children, offer them acceptable choices throughout the day.

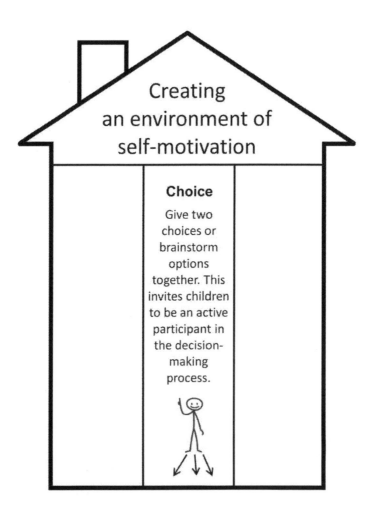

SELF-REFLECTION QUESTIONS:

1. *Is there a situation that frequently results in a battle with my child? If so, what is it?*

2. *What acceptable choices can I offer in this situation to avoid the battle?*

3. *Can my child take part in finding choices?*

4. *What are three other situations where I can offer my child choices?*

06

Competence

There is nothing noble in being superior

to your fellow man; true nobility

is being superior to your former self.

—Ernest Hemingway

It was a sweltering, humid day in middle Georgia. My husband David, our nine-year-old son Andrew, and I changed into our swimming suits and headed to the local pool. After thirty minutes of cooling off (Whew!), Andrew announced, "Dad, I've never learned how to dive; I want to learn how to dive."

"What? You've never learned how to dive?" David answered in surprise.

Andrew paused. I could sense his nervousness. "Actually I don't want to learn," he timidly replied.

"I can teach you how to dive."

"No, I don't want to."

"You can learn. Get on the side of the pool, and I'll show you how."

Andrew cautiously climbed out and followed his dad's instructions. He knelt on one knee and lifted his hands over his head. Pausing, he leaned over the water and pushed off. His feet hit first followed by the rest of his body.

As his head surfaced, I could see the frustration creased across his eyebrows. "You can do this," I called out.

He swam over to us. Determination had replaced his frustration. As he climbed out of the pool, my husband gave him more pointers. He knelt down again, raised his hands, and pushed off.

As I watched Andrew try and try again, the thought came to me, *"He is trying to increase his competence—he wants to know how to dive."*

Just like Andrew longed to feel competent at diving, all children long for the feeling of competence. This means having the ability to successfully accomplish a task. Feeling competent in their abilities is a psychological and emotional need felt at their very core.

Dr. Laura Markham, a clinical psychologist and author of *Ahaparenting.com* explains this deep need:

Children who see themselves as competent and capable feel powerful. They are more likely to be resourceful, to believe in themselves, to attempt difficult challenges, and to exhibit resilience in the face of setbacks.[18]

Wanting to feel competent starts at a young age. Picture a one-year-old who is learning to walk. At first she clutches her parents' fingers as she takes unstable steps. Gradually she scoots around holding on to couches to steady herself. Then she takes a cautious, teetering step all alone. Throughout the process she topples over, but her parent gives encouragement as her walking skills develop.

Learning to walk is a big milestone, but it is easy to forget that children are learning new skills every day. These include:

1. Physical skills such as jumping, running, and balancing.
2. Emotional skills like self-regulation, stress management, and coping with trauma.
3. Mental skills such as memorization, problem solving, and academic learning.
4. Social skills such as communication, building friendships, and team collaboration.
5. Life skills such as cooking, personal hygiene, and wellness.

With so many chances to develop competence, what can be the biggest obstacle? The same well intentioned people who can help—parents.

Don't Take Over !!!!

One of our responsibilities as parents is to keep our children safe. However, if we spend too much time hovering, or try to make their lives easy by solving their problems, we stifle our children's developing competence.

Ashley Söderlund, a child development psychologist and blogger at *Nurture & Thrive,* points out what happens when we do too much for our children:

> *When we step in and do things for our children or fix things for them, we are depriving them of a chance to learn. And not only to learn the task or the skill, but also*

to manage the emotions that come along with challenge and stress.[19]

As Söderlund points out, it is important to let children learn to work through challenges. This not only increases their competence but also their motivation.

When I conducted my interviews, I asked the children how they felt when they worked hard at a task and figured it out. Here are a few replies:

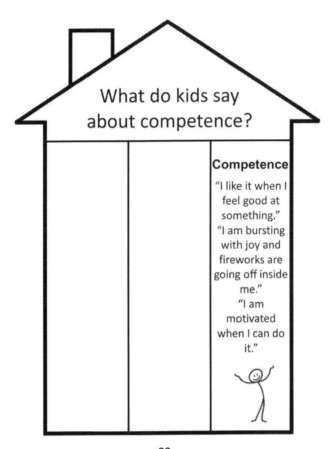

Children of all ages love learning new skills. They enjoy experiencing the feeling of competence. We need to encourage them to try—and help them succeed.

The Steps

Not sure what skills your children can learn? Let them guide you. If they show interest in a new skill, offer to teach them or show them how it is done.

Whenever possible, have them work alongside you in your yard and home. This can be called "elbow parenting" because your children work next to you, practicing and learning from your example.

Here are three steps to follow when teaching your children new skills:

1. Make sure whatever your children are learning is safe. Then monitor their progress by standing nearby without hovering over them.
2. Offer encouragement such as, "Keep trying," or "Look at you go!" If they struggle or hesitate, teach them the skills they are missing by demonstrating it in a new, simpler way so they can understand.
3. Let them practice as you monitor the situation. If they get tired or too discouraged, give them a break and come back to it later.

The more practice and experience children have, the more confident and competent they become.

Sadly, some parents ridicule or belittle their children when they are trying something new or practicing a skill.

Parents mistakenly think this motivates children, when in fact it does the exact opposite.

Children who feel discouraged or unsupported by parents stop trying, start whining, and feel vulnerable—which impedes an environment of self-motivation.

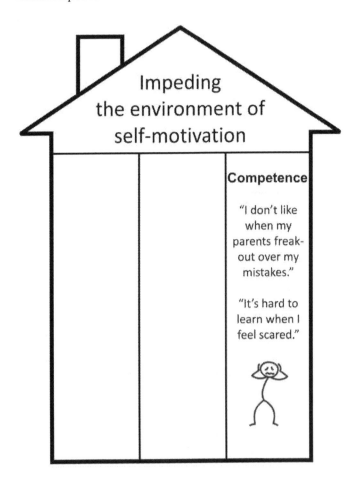

Remember the one-year-old who was learning to walk? Would we belittle her? No, of course not. Instead we clap, encourage, and smile so she continues trying. Similarly, children of all ages need guidance and encouragement from their parents as they learn and develop their new skills.

Just like learning to walk takes time and practice, so do all skills and milestones. Help your children gain the competence they need to succeed in life and feel good about themselves.

🏠 Creating the Environment

I loved watching Andrew learn to dive. He felt connected to his dad and knew he had a choice to keep trying. With each attempt, he got closer and closer to nailing a dive, and I could sense his growing confidence and competence.

After a few belly-flop setbacks (ouch), he finally achieved his first smooth dive. As his head emerged from under the water, his smile lit up the pool. Competence was written all over his face.

If you struggle with children not listening and being non-cooperative, spend time teaching them a new skill they want to learn. And as your children pass milestones and master new skills, point out what they accomplish. They will not only develop feelings of competence, but will also feel loved and a sense of belonging. This is the third step in creating an environment of self-motivation.

> **TAKE ACTION:** If you find yourself hovering over your child; step back, teach a skill, and let them practice.

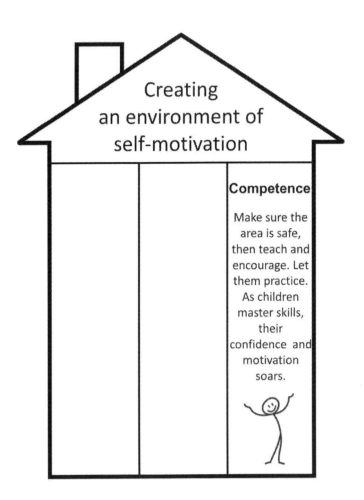

SELF-REFLECTION QUESTIONS:

1. *Is there a situation where I tend to hover over my child? If so, what is it? And is there a skill I can teach my child so he/she can independently complete the task?*

2. *What encouragement can I give my child the next time he/she is struggling to help him/her push through?*

3. *What are three new skills I can teach my child this week?*

Self-Motivated Kids

Part Three:
The Magic Formula

07

The Power of Three

One of the most important truths

is the power of three.

—**Author Unknown**

In Part 2: Creating the Environment, I shared a chapter on each of the three Cs and encouraged you to do the following:

1. Make time to *connect* with your children on their level.
2. Offer age-appropriate *choices* or discuss options when possible.
3. Teach skills to help your children develop *competence*.

Shianne, a mother of two young sons, has been meeting the needs of the three Cs in her home and shared these thoughts with me:

I have been using the three Cs with my kids and have noticed a night-and-day difference in their behavior. I find myself enjoying parenting more because I am able to connect with my kids and then see how happy they are when they get to choose something or accomplish something new.

Reading your examples made me realize there are so many opportunities to give choices. When I give a choice, I am connecting with my kids and giving them my time, which leads to happy feelings. Then when I compliment my kids or help them with a task, it makes them feel even better and more competent. Our lives have been extremely blessed by my kids' increased motivation.

As Shianne's thoughts explain, the three Cs are linked and closely related. Each time these needs are met, feelings of happiness are experienced by both the parent and child resulting in a more cooperative loving home.

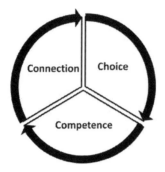

While you can interchangeably meet the needs of the three Cs, I discovered a 3 step formula that makes them most effective when you follow this order:

1. Connect with your child in a calm, kind way.
2. Give your child two choices or discuss your expectations.
3. Give encouragement or teach a missing skill so they can develop competence.

Here is an example of how this is done:

It's time to run errands and your daughter is playing with toys. You tell her it is time to go, and she starts throwing a fit. What do you do?

First connect! Give her a hug and acknowledge her point of view: "You really love playing with your toys."

Second, give her a choice by saying, "Which toy do you want to bring with you?" Let her pick the toy.

Third, help her develop competence by pointing out the listening skills she used: "Thank you for listening and following my instructions!"

What does your daughter experience with this approach? First, she feels supported and loved even though she had to stop playing and leave her toys. She still feels personal power because she was able to choose a toy to bring along. And she feels more competent because her listening skills were acknowledged.

No threats, manipulation, or bribes needed. Instead you created an environment where she was self-motivated and had the energy for action.

Six Strategies

Throughout my seventeen years of raising children and reading dozens and dozens of parenting books, I not only discovered the three Cs, but also six strategies that can consecutively meet the need for connection, choice, and competence.

These strategies are similar to a three-legged camping stool. When all three legs are intact, the stool functions effectively, holding the weight of a tired camper.

Likewise, each of the six strategies (explained in chapters 8-13) follows the magic formula of connection, choice, and competence which *effectively* create an environment of self-motivation.

I have personally tested the strategies in my home and interviewed children to understand their point of view. They really do work!

In each of the following chapters you will discover one strategy that creates an environment of self-motivation, along with a common parenting tactic that impedes self-motivation. Look for the house outlines to read what children have to say and a summary of how to implement the strategy so you can immediately start creating an environment of self-motivation in your home.

Ready to get started?

I'm so excited! Let's go!

Damara Simmons

08

Close, Quiet, Connect

The way we talk to our children becomes their inner voice.

—Peggy O'Mara

"Wow, it's getting late," I muse as I look at my watch. I glance over at my youngest son who is lying on the couch wrapped in a green blanket—like a snug pea in a pod.

"Can I stay up and sleep here?" he asks.

"Andrew, get upstairs. It is bedtime," I pronounce, as a mischievous grin flashes across his face. *Oh no, not tonight,* I think.

"Get moving," I holler from across the room.

Too often I find myself yelling when I am tired and my patience is gone. And I know I'm not alone.

In my interviewing, I found many parents are prone to yell when their kids fight, ignore instructions, or neglect their responsibilities. Yvonne, a mother of four young children, said:

I always end up yelling when my kids are supposed to be cleaning up or doing something I have asked them to do and [instead] continue to ignore me and run around chasing each other. Then one of my kids ends up getting hurt, and then I yell more.

Tiredness, lack of energy, irresponsibility, and children not listening are some reasons explosive parenting responses happen. Yelling might be a way to get our kids moving when our patience meter is drained, but it can cause harm.

According to a 2013 study published in the online journal *Child Development,* yelling—defined as shouting, cursing or insult-hurling—may be "just as detrimental" as physical punishment to the long-term well-being of teenagers. Yelling triggers feelings of low self-worth and depression in teens.[20]

When asked about parents' yelling and how it made them feel, the young children I interviewed said they felt scared, sad, or nervous. Teenagers said they felt angry because yelling was unfair and unnecessary.

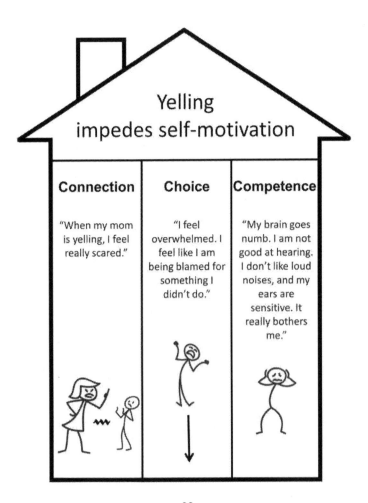

Yelling causes children to feel disconnected from their parents and triggers the reactive brain, which shuts down problem-solving and higher-thinking abilities. In summary, yelling impedes self-motivation.

Close, Quiet, Connect

My friend Laura shared this insightful comment about her personal shift away from yelling:

When my kids were little, I yelled because of tiredness, lack of response, to be heard, lack of alternative tools, and frustration. It wasn't until I read a great article that talked about how lowering your tone/voice, even to a whisper, was far more substantial. I still had moments, but they were fewer and further between, and my parenting frustrations were reduced substantially.

As Laura points out, communicating with your kids in a lowered voice is much more effective than yelling. This requires you to be in close proximity to your child. Reach out and place a gentle hand on your child. This physically connects you and catches your child's attention. You can think of it as *get close*, *be quiet*, and *connect*. The shortened mantra is "close, quiet, connect."

For example, when dinner is ready and you've told your kids to turn off the TV and come to the table, but they aren't listening, walk over to them and gently place your hands on their shoulders. Wait until you have eye contact and quietly say, "It's time for dinner. Turn off the show, and come sit down."

When you remain calm as you communicate with your children and speak in a quieter voice, they are able to listen and access their higher-level thinking. This in turn helps them process what you are requesting.

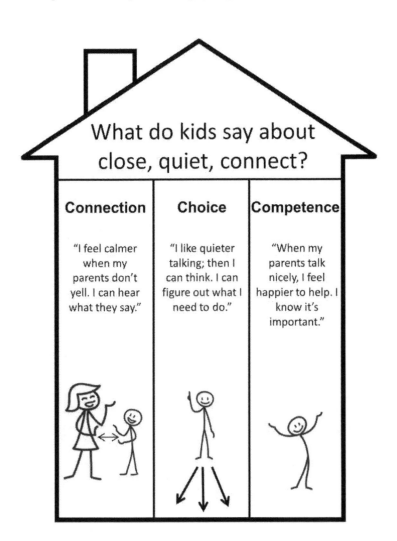

The Results

A number of moms have already tried the "close, quiet, connect" mantra. Amber, a busy mother of five, with children ranging from age six to twenty, shared what happened to her:

When I was calm and spoke quietly, everyone was calmer. They had to shush up so they could hear and understand me. After several days, we literally had no blow ups in the house. It made me realize how much control I really have as a parent without losing it. Even my kids mentioned, "You are really calm and reasonable."

Leah, a mother of a two-year-old and a five-year-old also tried the "close, quiet, connect" mantra. She shared these insights:

I feel like it's helped remind me that they're kids, and they just want to be happy and have fun. When I was close and calm, they responded more happily and quickly. Honestly, I was quite doubtful it would change things, but I have been VERY pleasantly surprised it has improved things on both ends!

As you can see, these two mothers were pleasantly surprised by the positive responsiveness of their children. Incorporating the mantra "close, quiet, connect" into your home environment can make a positive, loving difference.

🏠 Creating the Environment

When Andrew didn't want to go to bed, I took a deep breath and repeated to myself, *"Close, quiet, connect."* A liberating calm washed over me. I sat down on the couch next to him, softly placing my hand on his shoulder.

"Andrew it is bedtime," I said. I gently helped him up, and he scurried up the stairs. Whew! Crisis averted. Relationship intact.

When you get close, speak quietly, and connect with your children, you are meeting their need for the three Cs. Here is how it works: Say you need your daughter to come help with chores, but she is doing her homework. You walk over to her thinking *close, quiet, connect*. As you place a hand on her shoulder, gently say, "I see you are doing homework." Pause. "I need your help with some chores. Do you want to finish the problem you're on and then come help, or would you like to come now?"

The need for connection was met when you gently touched your daughter, spoke calmly and acknowledged what she was doing. You stated what needed to be done and offered a choice that honors her need to finish her homework problem. Asking your daughter to be a contributing family member and allowing her to finish her homework problem helps her develop competence in both those areas.

As you follow the steps of close, quiet, connect and meet your child's need for the three Cs, you are creating an environment of self-motivation in your home.

> **TAKE ACTION:** If you struggle with yelling at your kids, try the mantra "close, quiet, connect" to communicate what needs to be done.

Close, quiet, connect creates an environment of self-motivation

Connection

When you need your children to do something, get close, place a hand on their shoulder, and speak quietly so they feel connected and open to listening.

Choice

As you quietly point out the options your children have or discuss your expectations, you are meeting their need for choice.

Competence

When children are spoken to quietly, they do not feel attacked. Now they can access their higher-level thinking which helps them move forward with the task they are given.

SELF-REFLECTION QUESTIONS:

1. In what situations do I yell at my children?

2. What can I do instead?

3. The next time I feel like yelling at my kids, what can I do to remember the mantra "close, quiet, connect"?

Damara Simmons

09

What You *Can* Do

We spend all our energy telling them what

NOT to do, and they are never taught

what to do instead.

—Stacey Sly

The first page of the book *No, David!* by David Shannon, shows young David coloring all over the wall and his mother with her hands on her hips saying, "No, David, no!"

The book then follows David throughout his day as he reaches for the cookie jar, picks his nose, plays with his food, and spills water out of the bathtub. His mother is constantly calling out, "Stop that, David" or "No, David!"

Although the story is entertaining and the illustrations are amusing, it glaringly points out a huge communication issue. See if you can spot the problem as you read through this list:

> No dessert!
> Quit being so slow!
> Stop running!
> Don't hit!
> Stop climbing!
> Don't make a mess!
> Don't spill!
> Quit arguing!

What is the problem? Parents spend a lot of time stopping their child's behaviors, but don't take the time to explain what to do instead.

Behavioral Void

Dr. Rene Hackney, a school and developmental psychologist explains, "If children are unable to turn the negative language around to figure out the opposite, you have left them with what is called a behavioral void."[21]

Let's go back to the book, *No, David*. When his mother finds him coloring on the wall and simply tells him no, he experiences a behavioral void. Not knowing what to do instead, he returns to the unwanted behavior. Obviously these negative commands impede the environment of self-motivation. Here are a few thoughts shared by the insightful children:

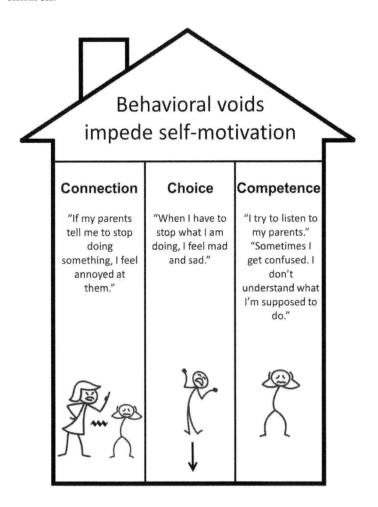

Positive Action

Marshall Rosenberg, a clinical psychologist and author of *Living Nonviolent Communication* suggests that "requests be expressed in positive-action language by stating clearly what we do want done."[22] This means we need to think, "What is it I want my child to do?" Then tell him the expectation in a positive way.

When David is coloring on the wall, what does his mom need him to do? She needs him to color on paper, not the walls. She communicates this by saying, "It is not okay to color on the wall. You can color on the paper like this."

When you clearly explain (using few words) what your children *can* do (using positive-action language), their higher-level thinking is activated. This encourages children to cooperate and is another strategy to create an environment of self-motivation.

When I asked children how they felt about being told to complete one simple task, they agreed that was far more effective than telling them to stop their current activity.

Here are a few thoughts they shared:

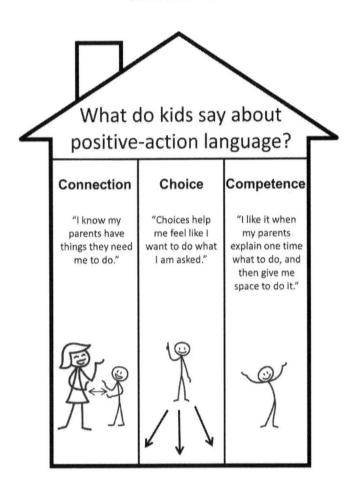

As you can see, children are receptive to positive-action language and more willingly cooperate because they know what they can do.

🏠 Creating the Environment

What else could David's mom say to him instead of constantly saying no and stop? How about, "David, use your fork and knife like this. David, blow your nose. David, turn the water off." Each of these positive-action responses teaches David what he can do, which sets him up for learning the appropriate behavior so he can repeat it in the future.

Speaking in positive-action language meets children's need for choice, connection, and competence. Here is an example:

Say you need your son to stop playing in his room and clean it up. You might feel like saying, "Stop playing around!" Instead, connect first by saying what you see and reminding him what needs to happen. This sounds like, "Looks like you are having lots of fun." Then, pat him on the back and smile, saying, "It's time to clean your room."

Next give him a choice: "Do you want to put your clothes away first or make your bed?" To help him develop feelings of competence ask, "Do you want me to help you get started?" If he starts cleaning on his own, point it out by saying, "Look at you cleaning!"

Speaking in positive-action language meets your child's need for the three Cs. When children know what they can do, you are helping create an environment of self-motivation.

> TAKE ACTION: If you struggle with getting your children to listen, use positive-action statements to guide them toward an acceptable solution.

Positive-action language creates an environment of self-motivation

Connection

Get close to your children when you make a request. Have them look you in the eyes. Calmly explain what needs to be done.

Choice

Offer children two acceptable choices such as, "You can clean your room first or help in the kitchen."

Competence

When you explain what needs to be done and help your children master the skills needed to complete the task, they are developing competence.

SELF-REFLECTION QUESTIONS:

1. *Do I often say the words stop, quit, don't, and no to my children?*

2. *When does this happen most often?*

3. *What can I say using positive-action language to explain what they need to do?*

4. *What positive-action phrases can I use every day?*

10

"The Why" Matters

If you want to build a ship, don't drum up the men to gather wood, divide the work, and give orders. Instead, teach them to yearn for the vast and endless sea.

—Antoine de Saint-Exupéry

In my parenting classes, I pose this question: "Imagine you ask your son to complete a chore and he responds, 'Why do I have to do that?' How would you reply?"

More often than not, the first response is "Because I said so!" And I understand why. When we need tasks completed, it's one of the easiest and quickest answers to give.

Now pause. When you were a kid, would this statement ignite a feeling of willing cooperation? Here are what kids had to say:

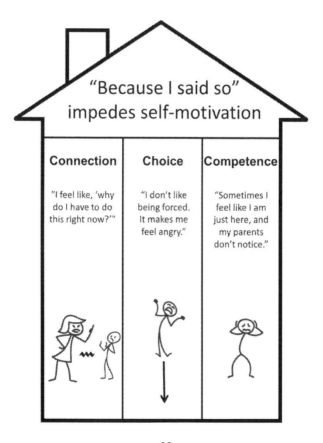

As you can see, this comment fails to create an environment of self-motivation. Instead it produces the opposite feeling: resistance. So what can you do?

"The Why"

In his TEDx talk, Dr. Edward Deci explains that self-motivation increases when we understand the *value or belief* behind what is being said. It helps us *see the big picture*.[23] This is *"the why."*

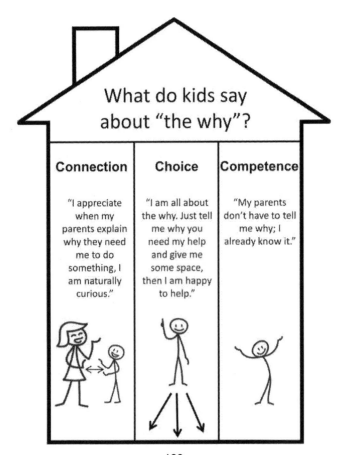

"The why" matters to children because it helps them understand that their contributions matters. It shows children the big picture, which in turn increases their self-motivation.

"Family Why"

Sinek explains this idea further: "Only when the WHY is clear and when people believe what you believe can a true loyal relationship develop."[24] In his book, Sinek addresses the company/customer relationship, but I believe it relates to family relationships as well. When your children believe they are important and are taught the values of your family, it gives them the opportunity to align their values with yours.

After thinking about this, I realized many of the tasks and activities I do with my family must seem random and haphazard. They needed to clearly understand what we believed.

While having dinner I asked, "What is important to our family? Why do we do what we do?" Each member called out his ideas. Then, after the brainstorming session, we had a quick discussion. Our final "why" list looked like this:

1. Learn all we can so we can become independent, successful adults.
2. Earn and save money so we can be self-reliant and help others.
3. Live the gospel of Jesus Christ so we are moral, joyful human beings.
4. Value each other because we are each unique individuals.
5. Be responsible for ourselves, our things, our behavior, and treatment of others.

6. Work together, help each other, and be a team because we need each other.
7. Serve and help others because our contribution matters.
8. Go on adventures because they are the spice of life.

After creating the list, I asked my children, "Does this help you understand why we ask you to do certain things?" They nodded.

"Why do we pick up after ourselves?" I asked.

"Because we are responsible for our things," my nine year-old son, Andrew replied.

"Exactly! Why do we chip in and help?"

"Because we are team and help each other out," exclaimed my thirteen-year-old son, Stephen.

"Yep! Why do we speak kindly to each other?"

"We value each other," replied my sixteen-year-old son Benjamin.

"Why don't we buy everything we want?"

"Because we want to save and be self-reliant," Stephen answered.

"Lastly, why do we go to school and work on projects here at home?"

"Because we want to better our lives and learning is awesome," yelled Andrew.

I enjoyed writing this list with my family, and it was very insightful. Charting the big picture of our family values allows each of us to catch the vision behind what we do and "why" we do it.

🏠 Creating the Environment

Instead of saying "Because I said so," I now remind my children of "the why." It is short and sweet, and my children get it (at least most of the time).

Defining and sharing "the why" with your family also meets the core needs of choice, connection, and competence. As you invite your children to share their ideas about "the why," your family discussion will foster connection and a feeling of belonging. And when children understand their specific roles and what is expected of them, their competence is developing.

You can refer back to your family "why" list as often as needed. If children question why they need to complete a task, remind them of your family values. When children understand "the why" of your family, you are painting the big picture of understanding and taking steps to create an environment of self-motivation.

> **TAKE ACTION:** If you regularly struggle with resistant children, take a few minutes to discuss "the why" of your family.

"The why" creates an environment of self-motivation

Connection

During a calm time, discuss your family values. Listen to your children and share your ideas.

Choice

Ask your children why the family values are important. This helps them align their belief system with yours.

Competence

When you need your children to complete a task remind them of the "why" or ask, "Why do you think it is important to our family?"

SELF-REFLECTION QUESTIONS:

1. *What do I say to my children when they are resistant?*

2. *What "why" can I explain instead?*

3. *What values are important to my family?*

4. *What day and time can I create my own family "why" list?*

11

Routines Reduce Friction

Friction is what makes the seemingly simple difficult, and the difficult impossible.

—Marine Corps Warfighting Pamphlet 1

"Let's go. We need to leave for church," I call out.

As I rush down the hallway, I discover my nine-year-old sitting on the floor playing with a toy.

"Andrew what are you doing? We need to leave. Get your clothes on," I whine.

When I hurry past my sixteen-year-old's room, I see him scrambling to grab his shoes.

"Come on, Benjamin!" I bark, "We need to go!" *It sure seems like children slow down when we need them to speed up!*

I was curious about how children feel when they are rushed along at a hurried pace. I posed this question to the kids I interviewed. Many echoed what fifteen-year-old Audrey explained: "When I am rushed and have to do a lot of things, I feel stressed that I have to do all of it in a short amount of time. It makes it hard to remember everything I have to do."

The younger children explained that mornings are extra difficult because they are so tired. This is what nine-year-old Anna shared:

When I am rushed and told to do many things in the morning, I feel tired. I have to get ready at 7:30 a.m. . . . I feel really, really tired. I feel scared when my mom yells out, and my brain gets overwhelmed.

As you can see, children feel disconnected from their parents when their parents yell at them. They also struggle with getting ready and remembering too many tasks. Here are additional comments from children about how rushing chaos makes them feel:

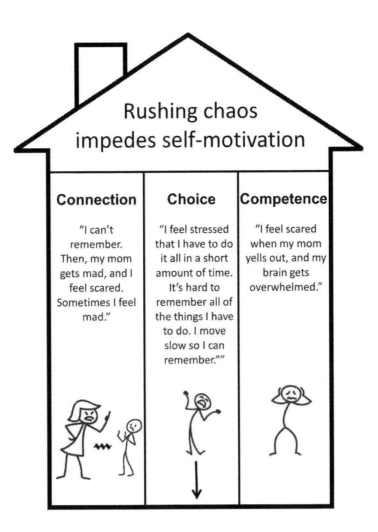

Rushing chaos triggers children's fight, flight, or freeze brain, which means they are merely trying to survive instead of listening and problem solving. As a result, children move slower and parents become more impatient and angry, which sadly causes the cycle to worsen.

Routines

So what is the answer to this rushing chaos? Establishing routines. If you are extremely busy, this might sound like one more thing to do, but research proves routines are worth incorporating into your family life.

Marshall Goldsmith, a personal coach for top business executives around the world and author of *Triggers,* explains the importance of routines this way:

> *Structure is how we overcome depletion. In an almost magical way, structure slows down how fast our discipline and self-control disappear. When we have structure, we don't have to make as many choices; we just follow the plan. And the net result is we're not being depleted as quickly.*[25]

Simply said, establishing routines creates structure in your home. It increases self-control and conserves energy for *both* you *and* your children. Without routines, all the decisions in daily life can overwhelm us.

I remember standing in my grandpa's machine shop as he showed me his lathe and other expensive equipment. He gently explained that in order for the machines to perform, it was essential to keep the moving parts well oiled. Otherwise, the machine would seize up and possibly break, costing extra energy, time, and money to fix. Just a few drops of oil made all the difference.

Similarly, our families can seize up and cost us extra time and energy when there is random chaos with unknown expectations. On the other hand, a few simple routines help our family life run more smoothly, like a few drops of oil.

Not only do routines help businesses and families run more smoothly, they are paramount in the military and dubbed *Standard Operating Procedures*.

Marine Captain Kevin Stephensen shared that routines are vital for the military and further explained, "Establishing *Standard Operating Procedures* is big in the military. They reduce friction and allow everyone to know what to do because it is a recognized routine."

Routines are essential in the military to ensure everyone knows their responsibilities, including what they are expected to do and when and where it will be completed. Lives depend on these well-practiced routines.

So what do children have to say about routines? Let's take a look:

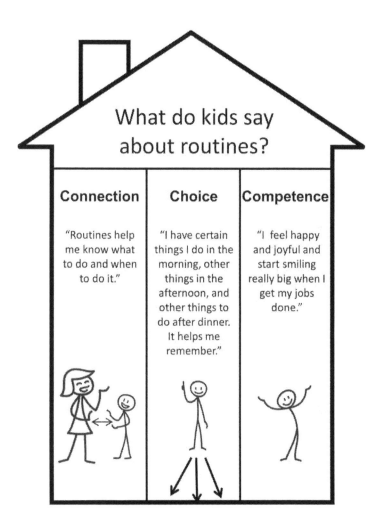

Although your family members' lives don't depend on routines, your relationships might. When everyone understands what is happening—along with their personal responsibilities—friction is reduced, higher-thinking is activated, and cooperation increases.

Chart and Practice

Where do you start? First ask yourself, "What time of day do I feel most impatient? When do we experience the most friction in our family?" Whatever time of day you identify, this is where a routine is needed.

Next, it is time to brainstorm as a family and decide what the routine should look like. Jane Nelson—a psychologist, educator, and author of *Positive Discipline*—points out, "Routines are especially effective when children have helped plan them."[26]

Then chart the routine so the entire family can see it. This is a visual reminder for everyone as you are learning the new routine. Below is an example to use with younger children for bedtime:

7:00	7:30	7:40	7:45	8:00
Baths	Pajamas on	Brush teeth & drink of water	Stories	Bedtime

If you have young children who cannot read, assign one task to each of their five fingers. This means bath time is assigned to the thumb, pajamas is assigned to the pointer finger, brushing teeth is assigned to the middle finger, and so on. You can even call it their "bedtime five" as a quick reminder.

The final step, and unfortunately the most overlooked, is to practice the routine. Take a few minutes to actually walk through what it looks like. This helps work out any bugs and starts committing it to memory. Then try the routine for a week and discuss the progress and results, making adjustments as needed.

Instead of rushing chaos, establish routines that make family life more predictable and peaceful for everyone.

🏠 Creating the Environment

After too many frantic Sunday mornings, I knew we needed a routine. We quickly made a list of what needed to happen on Saturday evening to prepare and what was expected Sunday morning. This is what it looked like:

Saturday evening:

>Check that church clothes are washed and ironed.
>Set alarm clock for 7:45.

Sunday morning:

>7:45 get up
>7:50 eat breakfast
>8:10 get dressed (all the way to shoes and socks)
>8:20 brush teeth
>8:30 walk out the door

Setting up a routine—so my children clearly understood what was expected—has helped our Sunday mornings run more smoothly. When the rushing chaos cycle starts again, it is time to review and practice because it is always a work in progress!

Charting and practicing routines in your home will meet your child's need for the three Cs. Routines increase connection as you calmly work toward the same goals and discuss what is expected. When children are involved in the discussion and planning of routines, the need for choice is being met. Routines also increase children's competence as they practice life skills such as, time management and personal hygiene.

Not only do routines meet your children's need for the three Cs, they reduce friction and chaotic rushing. In summary, they are another step in creating an environment of self-motivation.

> TAKE ACTION: If you are struggling with a specific time of day that feels chaotic and rushed, use a routine instead.

Routines create an environment of self-motivation

Connection	Choice	Competence
Discuss the benefits of a routine with your children. Calmly brainstorm ideas for high friction times.	Allow children to offer their ideas about the routine. Listen to their point of view.	Chart and practice the routine so children understand what needs to happen for the routine to be successful.

SELF-REFLECTION QUESTIONS:

1. *Are there times in my day when we experience more friction in our home?*

2. *What routine can I establish to make that time flow more smoothly?*

3. *How can I involve my children in charting out the routine?*

4. *When can we practice the routine?*

Damara Simmons

12

Transitions Allow Space

Life is pleasant. Death is peaceful.

It's the transitions that are troublesome.

—Matthew Arnold

My three sons Benjamin, Stephen, and Andrew love playing computer and iPad games. And often, they are playing when I need them to come for dinner or get started on their homework. When I am in a hurry, I find myself calling out, "Turn it off!" And as a result, they feel frustrated and angry at my immediate, commanding tone of voice.

Because parents keep family life running, we have an endless list of things to do and places to go. The demands never end. And because of this pressure, we might expect our kids to listen and immediately comply with our commands. We might even revert to being an army drill sergeant, barking out orders to our little "soldiers":

>Wake up!
>
>Get out of bed!
>
>Stop fighting!
>
>Clean your room!
>
>Finish your homework!
>
>Set the table!
>
>Clear the table!
>
>Go to bed!

I asked the children I interviewed, "How do you feel when you are doing an activity and are interrupted by a parent and told to do something else?" Here are a few comments:

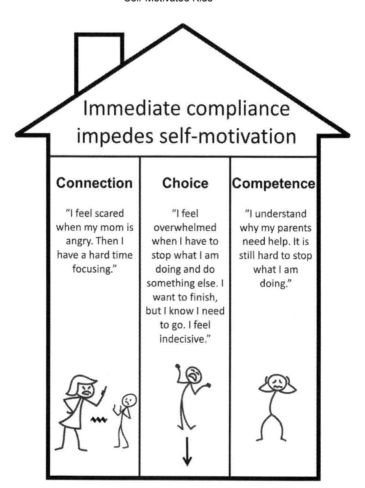

Clearly, children feel annoyed and hesitant when they are involved in an activity and are told to do something else.

Transitions

Instead of calling out orders expecting immediate compliance, we can give children transition cues to help them wind up what they are doing and move to the next activity.

The Center on the Social and Emotional Foundations for Early Learning reported:

> *Strategies that support smooth transitions between activities include verbal cues such as verbal reminders before transitions (e.g., "Five minutes before snack time," or "It's almost time to clean up.") and positive feedback after transitions.*[27]

This means when you need your children to do something, first communicate that a transition is coming. Tell them to finish what they are doing in the next two to three minutes, and then come help. Here are a few examples:

If you are at the park and it is time to go say, "We need to go. Do you want to go down the slide two or three more times?"

If you need your teenager to come help, ask, "How much time do you need to finish what you are doing?" Agree on a reasonable amount of time. Then give him space to finish up. When his time has passed, let him know it is time to move on.

After your children transition, thank them for finishing up and following through.

Effective transitions help your children's brains move from their current activity to the next. If they act out, reassure them they can continue the activity later that day or another time.

Here are a few thoughts from the children about transitions:

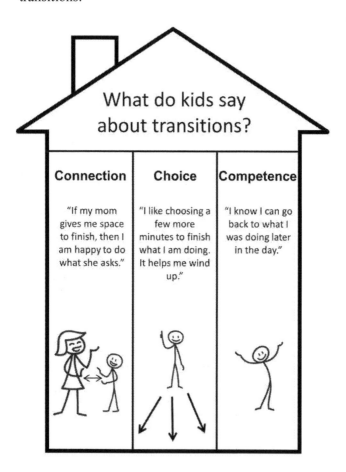

🏠 Creating the Environment

Giving children transition time meets their need for the three Cs. When children can choose between two amounts of time (two or three minutes) to finish up, they know you understand their point of view, which also increases feelings of connection. And when they transition between tasks, they are developing competence in their abilities.

I have learned to use transitions when my sons are playing on the computer or iPad and our conversation sounds something like this:

"Stephen I need your help with dinner. How much time do you need to finish?

"Maybe three more minutes," Stephen replies.

"Okay, I need you in the kitchen in three minutes."

When I use transitions, my sons appreciate the space and more willingly cooperate. And because it helps them feel respected, it creates an environment of self-motivation.

> TAKE ACTION: If you are struggling with resistant children, give them time to transition from one activity to another.

Transitions create an environment of self-motivation

Connection

When you need your children to stop what they are doing and complete another task, offer a transition time.

Choice

Offer two transition times and let your children choose, so they feel some control in their lives.

Competence

Tell your children they can return to their activity at another time. This helps them work through their disappointment.

SELF-REFLECTION QUESTIONS:

1. *Do I experience resistance when my child needs to move from one activity to another?*

2. *How do I normally react? Do I expect immediate compliance?*

3. *What transition could I use instead?*

13

Engaging Questions

On some level we must know…

that questions are important and that we should

be paying more attention to them—

especially the meaningful ones.

—Warren Burger

In the book *Will it Fly?,* author Pat Flynn teaches his young son Keoni how to fold and fly paper airplanes. Keoni excitedly rushes into the task, but his plane bombs, inducing him to give up.

Instead Pat asks, "Why do you think your plane didn't fly like mine?"

Keoni answers that his dad's was better.

Pat then asks, "What about my plane was better?" Keoni is unsure, so Pat shows him his plane and asks another question: "What do you see on my plane that you think makes it fly?" They then discuss the need for two wings that work— something Keoni doesn't yet know how to make. The entire time, Pat continues asking his son questions.

Now contrast this story with parents who lecture their children. In fact, remember how in the Charlie Brown cartoons the adults are never pictured? Instead, Charlie Brown looks off-screen while having a conversation with a parent who sounds like "Muh muh ma muh." It is garbled and impossible to understand—like noise.

Likewise, when we lecture our children, we sound like noise. It's easy for this to happen because we want to get a point across and feel the need to repeat ourselves over and over until our children finally "get it." But this is lecturing. And as the children I interviewed reveal, it impedes self-motivation:

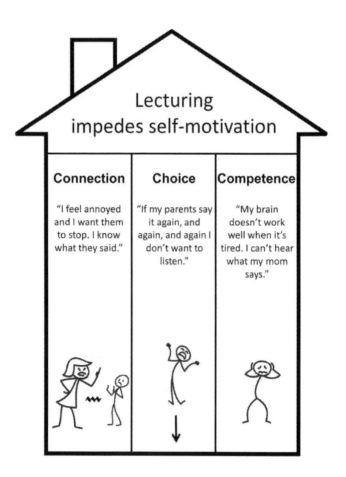

As you can see from their comments, lecturing our children does not help them become more responsive (like we want), it causes the opposite reaction: resistance.

Ask Engaging Questions

My sixteen-year-old son, Benjamin recently explained how much he enjoys teachers who ask thought-provoking questions and lead discussions instead of merely lecturing. I agree with him.

Engaging, thought-provoking questions pique our interest and require us to process information on a deeper level. Questions invite us to be active learners.

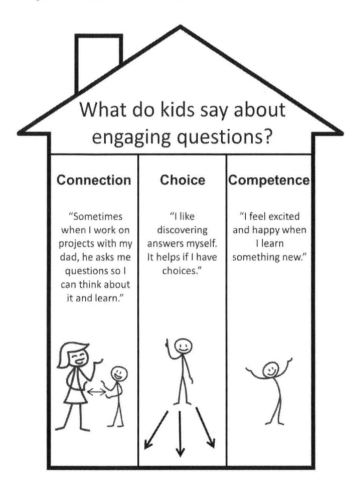

Amy Morin, a licensed clinical social worker and psychotherapist, shares that "*asking the right question* is the key to behavior change." Research shows that asking a question about future behavior increases a person's motivation to change.[28]

The Steps

Think of what you need your children to do. Instead of lecturing, ask a question. For example, "Do you want to go out to play? What tasks need to be finished first?" Be sure your body language and tone of voice are calm and friendly so children don't feel threatened or fearful, which shuts down their higher-level thinking.

After asking your child an engaging question, allow him time to answer and brainstorm possible solutions. If needed, give him a reassuring hug or pat on the back, signaling that you believe in his ability. It is quick and easy—no long lecture needed.

Instead of:	*Say This:*
Go make your bed, brush your teeth, comb your hair.	What are the five things you need to do this morning?
You need to practice the piano now.	What do you need to do before you play?
You need to get this done.	What is stopping you from doing this job?

You can use engaging questions to redirect children towards tasks they need to complete. However, you can also use them when a child makes a mistake: "What did you learn from this situation?" Or if your child is struggling with a project or class, you can ask, "Did you do your best? What could you improve?"

When parents calmly ask engaging questions, children become active learners, which increases their motivation. Questions give children the opportunity to discover their own answers and be involved in solving their own problems.

🏠 Creating the Environment

Can asking engaging questions create an environment of self-motivation in your home? Yes—yes it can.

Connect with your child by squatting down on his level and getting close. Smile and ask open-ended questions in a friendly tone so he can think and learn. If he is unsure how to proceed, give him a choice that encourages him to choose an idea and move into action. When your child learns how to solve his own problems through the process of questions, he develops feelings of competence and learns he is capable.

Pat used engaging questions to help Keoni discover how to fold a new and improved paper airplane. After he launched it and watched it soar, Keoni screamed with excitement, "Dad, can you believe it did that?" Now that's what parenting is all about and no lecture was needed.

> TAKE ACTION: If you struggle with lecturing your children, think about what your child needs to do; then ask an engaging question.

Engaging questions create an environment of self-motivation

Connection

Sit next to your children. Speak in a calm, friendly tone. Ask open-ended questions that invite children to think about their own solutions.

Choice

Offer choices if children struggle finding their own solutions. Choices can be phrased as questions.

Competence

Questions help children develop problem solving skills. They encourage children to creatively think about solutions and move to action.

SELF-REFLECTION QUESTIONS:

1. *Do I lecture my children?*

2. *Which phrases or commands do I say over and over?*

3. *Instead of these lectures or commands, what questions can I ask my child to invite action?*

4. *What are three questions I can use during my child's bedtime routine or other during other sticky parts of the day?*

Self-Motivated Kids

Part Four:
Where to Start?

14

The Gift of Today

Life can only be understood backwards,

but it must be lived forward.

—**Soren Kierkegaard**

During spring break of 2016, my family and I spent time in the Appalachian Mountains. We hiked along dirt trails and through miles of green forests in search of majestic waterfalls. My feet were aching by the end of each day, but a feeling of deep satisfaction filled me from the tips of my toes to the top of my head.

Just like a hike begins with one step and then another, our parenting journey beings with one step and then another. Reading this book and putting into action some of the ideas are steps in your *personal* journey.

Where do you start? Below is an overview of the chapters. I suggest you choose an area you want to improve and start there.

- Chapter 4 – Instead of letting busyness and impatience take over your life, scale back your activities and spend quality connection time with your children.
- Chapter 5 – Instead of asserting "my way or the highway," give your children choices.
- Chapter 6 – Instead of doing too much for your children, teach them skills so they develop feelings of competence.
- Chapter 8 – Instead of yelling, move close, get quiet, and connect with your children as you tell them what is expected.
- Chapter 9 – Instead of telling your children what they can't do, tell them what they *can* do.
- Chapter 10 – Instead of saying "because I said so," share the "why."

- Chapter 11 – Instead of randomly going through your day, establish routines everyone can count on and work towards.
- Chapter 12 – Instead of having the "do it now" attitude, give your children transition cues.
- Chapter 13 – Instead of lecturing to your children, ask them engaging questions and brainstorm solutions together.

After you decide which strategy to start with, read the self-reflection questions at the end of the chapter. Answer them honestly and make a plan. Then put it into action.

If you are still unsure where to begin, start with connection. Your children need to feel love and belonging from you every day.

When I outline the skills needed to create an environment of self-motivation, many parents say they have already tried some of the strategies. I say, "That's great! Keep trying!"

An environment of self-motivation is not created in a day. It is created when feelings of connection, choice, and competence are experienced by children *every day.*

In this new home environment there are no threats, coercive comments or punishments meant to harm. There are no bribes or guilt-trips. Instead it is a place where your children feel safe, loved, and cared for. Where their needs are respected and met.

So what is the outcome? Children who think creatively for solutions, make positive contributions in your home, enjoy learning, willingly cooperate, and listen. In summary, *they become self-motivated kids!*

Want kids who have the energy for action? Want to create an environment of self-motivation in your home? Pick one of the chapters and start using the strategies and language *today*.

You've got this! You're AWESOME!

As Dr. Seuss said, "Today is your day. You're off to great places! You're off and away!"

15

Don't Take My Word for It

Pretty much all the honest truth telling

in the world is done by children.

—Oliver Wendell Holmes

When I considered writing a parenting book I wanted it to be unique and fresh. That's when the idea to interview children came to mind.

Where can I find children to interview? I wondered. *Of course! Most my friends on Facebook have children.* "Who has children I could interview for my book?" I posted. Immediately, responses poured in.

The time I spent talking with these children was enlightening. Their ages range from 3- 17. Hearing their points of view opened my mind as a mom and parent educator.

If you need motivation to make adjustments in your parenting and understand your children on a deeper level, ask them these questions. Maybe enjoy a cup of hot chocolate or a bowl of ice cream as you have a heart-to-heart discussion. I guarantee you will not regret it.

1. What is something you fear?
2. How do you push through the fear?
3. How do you feel when you are rushed?
4. Can you remember everything you need to do?
5. Do you enjoy having choices?
6. Do choices help you feel more motivated?
7. What makes you feel loved?
8. Can you listen more when I speak quietly or yell?
9. What makes it difficult for you to listen?
10. Do you enjoy learning new skills?
11. What is something you would like to learn or do together?
12. What makes you feel proud of yourself?

13. Do you like knowing "why" I ask you to do something? Does that help you feel more motivated?
14. Does a routine help you remember what to do?
15. Do you like having a few minutes to wind up what you are doing before moving to a new task?
16. Do I lecture? What does it sound like?
17. What is the hardest thing about being a kid?

Now what? Think about the answers. Relish what they mean. They are sweet gifts to you!

Ready to start creating the environment of self-motivation in your home? You can do it! If you need help, send me an email anytime: damara@selfmotivatedkids.com

Looking back to 1999, when my sweet newborn son was placed in my arms, I wish I had this book. Instead, it is my gift to YOU.

With much love,

Damara

Where Do You Go From Here?

My website and articles at ParentingBrilliantly.com were created to help parents like you! That's where I share more stories and strategies from my own life and research. All of the information on the website is free, so check it out. I look forward to serving you there!

Cheers, and here's to you and your success! If you'd like to let me know what you thought of this book, shoot me a message at damara@parentingbrilliantly.com. Thanks again!

One last thing. If you enjoyed this book or found it helpful, I would be very grateful if you posted a short review on Amazon. Your support really does make a difference and I read all the reviews personally so I can get your feedback and make this book even better.

Thank you for your support!

Self-Motivated Kids

Self-Motivated Kids Companion Course

THE SECRET IS OUT….

You can create a home environment where your children listen and cooperate. And you know how it is done!

Meet your child's 3 basic psychological needs.

To help you create this environment in your home, I designed a companion course for you at the following website:

SelfMotivatedKids.com/course

Although it is not required, I highly recommend the free e-course. You'll get access to additional materials, a supportive community, and a few surprises along the way.

Ready to implement what you have learned throughout this book? Ready to create an environment of self-motivation in your home? Need help doing it?

Join me in the e-course. Reserve your spot with this link:

SelfMotivatedKids.com/course

Additional Parenting Resources

Ideas are meant to be acted on, and I sincerely hope you are inspired to create an environment of self-motivation in your home. On the homepage of my website, Parenting Brilliantly, you can find links to help you with specific challenges you are facing.

ParentingBrilliantly.com

Click on the Blog button to find a table of contents page which has articles organized according to ages. Parents find this resource helpful and easy to use. I am regularly writing and adding more articles to help and inspire moms and dads.

Recommended Parenting Books & Websites

Peaceful Parent, Happy Kids

by Dr. Laura Markahm

This book guides you to foster emotional connection with your child which creates real and lasting change. When you have that vital connection, you don't need to threaten, nag, plead, bribe or even punish.

The Whole-Brain Child

by Daniel Siegel, M.D. & Tina Bryson, Ph.D.

This book shares 12 key strategies that foster healthy brain development, which leads to calmer, happier children.

How to Talk So Kids Will Listen &
Listen So Kids Will Talk

by Adele Faber & Elaine Mazlish

This best-selling book gives you the know-how you need to be more effective with your children and more supportive of yourself.

Positive Discipline

By Jane Nelsen, Ed.D

This book teaches that the key to positive discipline is not punishment, but mutual respect. It is the classic guide to helping children develop self-discipline, responsibility, cooperation, and problem-solving skills.

The Parenting Breakthrough

By Merrilee Browne Boyack

This book shares a real-life plan to teach your kids how to work, save money, and be truly independent.

ImperfectFamilies.com

By Nicole Schwartz, LMFT

This blog has insightful articles written by family therapist Nicole Schwartz. She is passionate about helping parents use positive, respectful strategies with their kids.

NurtureandThriveblog.com

By Ashley Söderlund, Ph.D.

This blog is written by child behavior psychologist Ashley Söderland who has a passion for understanding why kids develop the way they do. She helps parents understand emotions, behavior, communication, and connection.

TheParentingJunkie.com

This website by Avital provides various videos discussing parenting topics from timeouts to self-care. Her motto is "Love parenting and parent out of love."

Damara Simmons

Acknowledgements

I am deeply grateful to so many who shared their thoughts and talents to make this book a reality.

First, many thanks to **the children** I interviewed. Your insights were priceless: Bree, William, Emily, Genevieve, Savannah N., Evelyn, Audrey, Anna, Tyler, Elizabeth, Joey, Sam, Faith, Aaron, Savannah, Riley, Ella, Daryl, Jantzen, Logan, Ellie, Ezra, Micah, Sarah, Rachel, Ri-Lee, Kaden, Lily, Wyatt, Aspen, Lincoln, Easton, Luke, Jaycee, Nate, and Sadie.

Thank you to my **Book Launch Team** who gave suggestions, posted comments, and answered all my endless questions: Jessaca Olsen, Angela Trusty, April Neary, April Andreason, Rebecca Ahlquist, Becky Morrill, Cara Nelson, Courtney Conover, Debbie Davis, Diane Eber, Judy Stephensen, Elaine Horne, Felicia Dellis, Gabi Paleta, Jacquel Tholl, Jennifer Zimmerman, Jena Feutz, Jessica Meek, Kari Hansen, Kelly Cross, Kevin Stephensen, Leah Brown, Lisa Carlson, Lisa Juhasz, Mandy Campbell, Michelle Evans, Travis Stephensen, Nicole Burnham, Rachel Izu, Rachel Johnston, Randee McAffee, Shianne Healey, Stacey Sly, Stephanie Carlson, Stephanie Davis, Yeon Mi Hicken, Suzanna Peterson, and Yvonne Taylor.

Thank you to my **editing team**; you took my ideas and made them flow: Stephanie Carlson, Angela Trusty, Kevin Stephensen, and Stacey Sly.

Thank you to my **editor**, Sarah Monson, who understood my words and heart and made them become one.

Thank you to my **graphic designer**, Julie Brew Finlayson, who listened to my ideas and created a cover that shines.

Thank you to my **children** whose very presence inspires me to be a better person and mother.

Thank you to my **husband** whose wisdom, counsel, and encouragement propelled me forward on the days I wanted to quit.

Thank you to **God** for putting me on this path of learning so I could help others.

First love–my family.

Benjamin, David, Damara, Andrew, and Stephen

Second love–talking parents' ears off. ☺

About the Author

Damara Simmons has been a mother and researcher for over 17 years. Through her website, ParentingBrilliantly.com, she guides parents to find solutions to their parenting frustrations so they can stop feeling overwhelmed and start feeling calm and confident.

She has been featured on Family Share, KSL, Kid Spot, Power of Moms, and Jewish World Review.

She loves spending time with family and friends, especially if dark chocolate is involved. Damara enjoys going on adventures and being outside (except in the extreme heat). Reading books, laughing with family, and playing an occasional sport are a few of her favorite things.

Damara is a Certified Family Life Educator, and a member of the National Council of Family Relations. She currently lives in Bonaire, Georgia with her husband and three sons.

To learn more about Damara, go to:

ParentingBrilliantly.com/about

Notes

1 Pink, D. (2009). *Drive: The Surprising Truth About What Motivates Us*. New York: Penguin Group, 16.

2 Pink, D. (2009). *Drive: The Surprising Truth About What Motivates Us*. New York: Penguin Group, 17.

3 Sinek, S. (2009). *Start With Why: How Great Leaders Inspire Everyone To Take Action*. London: Penguin Books Ltd, 21.

4 Ryan, R. M., & Deci, E. L. (2000). Self-Determination Theory and the Facilitation of Intrinsic Motivation, Social Development, and Well-Being. American Psychologist, 68-78.

5 Sly, S. (2016). Trauma in the Classroom. Las Vegas: My Space, 112.

6 Ryan, R. M., & Deci, E. L. (2000). Self-Determination Theory and the Facilitation of Intrinsic Motivation, Social Development, and Well-Being. American Psychologist, 68-78.

7 Pink, D. (2009). *Drive: The Surprising Truth About What Motivates Us*. New York: Penguin Group, 87.

8 Hanh, T. N. (1992). *Peace is Every Step: The Path of Mindfulness*. New York: Bantam Books, 78.

9 Deci, E. L. (2012). *Promoting Motivation, Health, and Excellence*. TedxFlour City. Retrieved from http://tedxtalks.ted.com/video/Promoting-Motivation-Health-and;Health

10 Lieberman, M. D. (2013). *Social: Why Our Brains Are Wired To Connect*. New York: Broadway Books, 249.

11 Ryan, R. M., & Deci, E. L. (2000). Self-Determination Theory and the Facilitation of Intrinsic Motivation, Social Development, and Well-Being. American Psychologist, 68-78.

12 Grossman, S. (2008). *Offering Children Choices: Encouraging Autonomy and Learning While Minimizing Conflicts.* Early Childhood News. Retrieved from http://www.earlychildhoodnews.com/earlychildhood/article_view.aspx?ArticleID=607

13 Taylor, J. (2013). *Get Out of Your Children's Way to Build Competence.* Psychology Today. Retrieved from https://www.psychologytoday.com/blog/the-power-prime/201312/get-out-your-childrens-way-build-competence

14 McKeown, G. (2014). *Essentialism: The Disciplined Pursuit of Less.* New York: Crown Publishing.

15 Tsabary, S. (2013). *Out of Control.* Vancouver: Namaste Publishing, 43.

16 Stephensen, T. (2015). *Exploring Edges: Field Notes From Experiments in Medicine, Endurance Sports, and Love.* Create Space, *178.*

17 McKeown, G. (2014). *Essentialism: The Disciplined Pursuit of Less.* New York: Crown Publishing, 35.

18 Markham, L. *10 Tips to Raise a Competent Child.* Ahaparenting.com. Retrieved from http://www.ahaparenting.com/parenting-tools/emotional-intelligence/competence

19 Söderland, A. *Why Challenge is Important for Children's Emotional Intelligence.* Nurtureandthriveblog.com. Retrieved from http://nurtureandthriveblog.com/why-challenge-is-important-for-childrens-emotional-intelligence/

20 Wang, M.-T. and Kenny, S. (2014), *Longitudinal Links Between Fathers' and Mothers' Harsh Verbal Discipline and Adolescents' Conduct Problems and Depressive Symptoms.* Child Development, 85: 908–923. doi: 10.1111/cdev.12143

21 Hackney, R. (2013). *Give Children Positive Directions.* Parenting Answers. Retrieved from http://parentingbydrrene.com/2013/03/24/give-children-positive-directions/

22 Rosenberg, M. (2012). *Living Nonviolent Communication: Practical Tools to Connect and Communicate Skillfully in Every Situation.* Boulder: Sounds True, Inc., 13.

23 Deci, E. L. (2012). *Promoting Motivation, Health, and Excellence.* TedxFlour City. Retrieved from http://tedxtalks.ted.com/video/Promoting-Motivation-Health-and;Health

24 Sinek, S. (2009). *Start With Why: How Great Leaders Inspire Everyone To Take Action.* London: Penguin Books Ltd, 73.

25 Goldsmith, M. (2015). *Triggers: Creating Behavior That Lasts- Becoming The Person You Want To Be.* New York: Crown Business, 187.

26 Nelsen, J. (1981). *Positive Discipline: The Classic Guide To Helping Children Develop Self-Discipline, Responsibility, Cooperation, and Problem-Solving Skills.* New York: Random House, Inc., 268.

27 Ostrosky, M. M., Jung, E. Y., & Hemmeter, M. L. (n.d.). *Helping Children Make Transitions Between Activities.* Center on the Social and Emotional Foundations For Early Learning. Retrieved from http://csefel.vanderbilt.edu/briefs/wwb4.pdf

28 Morin, A. (2016). *The Surprising Trick to Get Someone (Or Yourself) to Change.* Psychology Today. Retrieved from https://www.psychologytoday.com/blog/what-mentally-strong-people-dont-do/201601/the-surprising-trick-get-someone-or-yourself-change

Made in the USA
Lexington, KY
07 May 2019